HEBREW IDOLATRY AND SUPERSTITION

HEBREW IDOLATRY AND SUPERSTITION:

ITS PLACE IN FOLK-LORE.

BY

ELFORD HIGGENS.

KENNIKAT PRESS
Port Washington, N. Y./London

HEBREW IDOLATRY AND SUPERSTITION

First published in 1893
Reissued in 1971 by Kennikat Press
Library of Congress Catalog Card No: 73-118527
ISBN 0-8046-1150-5

Manufactured by Taylor Publishing Company   Dallas, Texas

CONTENTS

CHAPTER I.

TRADITIONAL RELIGION.

CHAPTER II.

THE RELIGION OF THE SOIL.

CHAPTER III.

AMORITE RELIGION AND WORSHIP OF HEAVENLY BODIES.

CHAPTER IV.

DIVINATION, WITCHCRAFT, ENCHANTMENT.

CHAPTER V.

CONCLUSION.

126. More stress should be laid on influence of aborigines. — 127. The Hebrews would naturally adopt the idolatry around them.—128. Uncivilized people have tendency to be alarmed at unknown surroundings. — 129. The Israelites

HEBREW IDOLATRY AND SUPER-STITION

CHAPTER I.

TRADITIONAL RELIGION.

1. THE recent attempts to rewrite the early history of the Hebrews—in order to show that the national genius produced their remarkable religion by a gradual development from a period of the grossest barbarism—have not proved a success. There is not sufficient evidence produced to show that the early Hebrews *were* sunk in such degraded savagery. Dr. Tylor says : ' Civilization is a plant much oftener propagated than developed,' and the civilization and religion of the Hebrews, which are so nearly connected, are not proved to have been developed by the national genius.

2. Most attempts to prove this hypothesis base the strongest of their arguments upon

the constant references to idolatrous customs
practised by the Israelites during the periods
of the Kings and the Prophets, and it is suggested that they are survivals of the ancient
worship of the nation.   But it is most remarkable that in every place where mentioned these
idolatrous practices are sternly denounced, are
described as the religion of the former inhabitants of Palestine, and the Divine anger is
always threatened against those who practise
them.

3. In considering this subject, however, it
is impossible to ignore such a book as Professor Robertson Smith's ' Religion of the
Semites.'   It is undoubtedly a book of great
value in considering the early religion and
civilization of that race.   The writer makes
much use of folklore, but, like a great many
modern critics, prefers to ignore Moses and
the Prophets, and in doing so forsakes the
conclusions to which his folklore would take
him, and falls back on his own conjectures.

4. He says : ' Behind these positive religions '
(Judaism, Christianity, and Islam) ' lies the
old unconscious religious tradition, the body
of religious usage and belief, which cannot be
traced to the influence of individual minds,
and was not propagated on individual authority,

but formed part of that inheritance from the past into which successive generations of the Semitic race grew up as it were instinctively, taking it as a matter of course that they should believe and act as their fathers had done before them.'

5. That there was a body of traditional usage during a great portion of their history seems certain; but that it was an inheritance from the past generations of the Semitic race is not so certain.

6. In this country there are still surviving traditions and customs from pre-Aryan times. Is it certain that, at any rate, among the Hebrews, there were not similar traditions surviving from pre-Semitic times, and that the lapses to idolatry were not caused by the presence among the Hebrews of a non-Semitic race, or of a people practising customs derived from such a race?

7. The Psalmist says:

' They did not destroy the peoples,
 As the Lord commanded them ;
 But mingled themselves with the nations,
 And learned their works ;
 And they served their idols ;
 Which became a snare unto them :
 Yea, they sacrificed their sons and their daughters unto
  demons,

And shed innocent blood, even the blood of their sons
and of their daughters,
Whom they sacrificed unto the idols of Canaan ;
And the land was polluted with blood.
Thus they were defiled with their works,
And went a whoring in their doings.
Therefore was the wrath of God kindled against His
people.'

PSALM cvi. 34-40.

8. Now this is exactly the state of things
to which the evidence points. A foreign race
takes possession of Palestine, finds there an
idolatrous race, which they were commanded
to utterly exterminate. This they did not do.
They merely subjected them partially, and
settling down among them, learned their
customs and religion.

9. The writer of the Book of Wisdom de-
scribes this former race and their customs in
rather forcible language : ' For it was Thy
will to destroy by the hands of our fathers
both those old inhabitants of Thy holy land,
whom Thou hatedst for doing most odious
works of witchcrafts and wicked sacrifices ;
and also those merciless murderers of children
and devourers of man's flesh and the feasts
of blood, with their priests out of the midst
of their idolatrous crew, and the parents that
killed with their own hands souls destitute of
help ' (Wisdom xii. 3-6).

10. In this passage there appears to be a distinction drawn between two divisions of the ' old inhabitants.' This is important, and we will meet with the divisions again. There appear to be those who practise ' witchcrafts and wicked sacrifices,' and those who are ' murderers of children and devourers of man's flesh and the feasts of blood.' If we may anticipate what it is hoped to prove later on, we may class the former division as the Hittite and kindred races, while the latter division are the Amorites mixed with the earliest inhabitants of the land.

11. The command to utterly exterminate the aborigines of Palestine has often been looked upon as incompatible with the Divine attributes; but if the Hebrews were to be preserved from idolatry the complete extirpation of the heathen inhabitants appears a necessity. Professor Robertson Smith says justly (p. 336): ' Experience shows that primitive religious beliefs are practically indestructible except by the destruction of the race in which they are ingrained.' The truth of this statement is, I think, apparent to most students of custom and institution.

12. We must next proceed to ask what evidence there is to show that a people can

retain the customs and traditions of a former race, after such race appears to have died out or to have become absorbed in the conquering race. And if such a state of affairs exists now, is there any evidence that it existed in former times? If we can get an affirmative answer we can then account for the idolatrous lapses of the Hebrews as being merely the coming to the surface of the heathenism of the former inhabitants by whom the Hebrews were corrupted, and not 'an inheritance from the past into which successive generations of the Semitic race grew up,' and which was part of the primitive belief of their fathers.

13. Mr. Gomme, in his very interesting book, ' Ethnology in Folklore ' (chap. iv.), has shown that the dressing of wells in this country is a survival of well-worship dating from pre-Aryan times. He shows that in counties which were peopled by Teutons—the last Aryan invaders—the wells are simply reverenced and associated with the name of some saint. In counties inhabited by a mixed Celtic and Teutonic population the wells are used for divination, dressed with garlands, and are ' pin ' wells. While where the Celtic population was mixed with the pre-Aryan aborigines, the wells are used for the cure of diseases or for producing

rain, are provided with a rag-bush and have an animal genius in attendance. He also calls attention to the fact that if well-worship had been an Aryan custom, we would expect to find it in its most primitive form where the tribes of purest Aryan blood had settled, whereas it is just there where it is seen in its least distinctive form. And in those parts where the pre-Aryan inhabitants remained, the custom survives in its most archaic form.

14. In his 'Village Community,' Mr. Gomme also calls attention to various pre-Aryan survivals in modern folklore and custom, such as hill-terrace cultivation, harvest customs, the hearth cult, the periodical redistribution of the common lands, and many other customs which it is not necessary to specify.

15. That similar survivals were also found among the ancients can, I think, be shown. Mr. J. G. Frazer, in a paper read before the Cambridge branch of the Hellenic Society (published in *Folklore*, 1890), called attention to the fact that the 'Symbols of Pythagoras' were merely folklore which had survived amongst the Greek peasantry from prehistoric times, and the meaning of which had been lost, so that philosophers who tried to give a meaning to the 'Symbols' had to adopt some far-

fetched explanation in order to make them appear rational.

16. It is not, however, necessary to enter more fully into such evidence at present, for in considering in detail the idolatrous rites practised in Palestine, we will be able to draw parallels between such customs and those of other nations, and also trace the remains of such customs in modern folklore. But I think sufficient has been said to show that in the opinion of competent judges there are in our own highly-civilized country traces still left of its occupation by a non-Aryan aboriginal race, and that the researches of scholars are also bringing to light evidence of a similar state of things in other countries.

17. Before considering the idolatrous customs among the Hebrews, however, let us see what heathen nations were left in Palestine.

Beginning at the north, we find that around Sidon, on the slopes of Lebanon and Hermon, at Achzib, Bethanath, Ahlab, and around Accho, the former inhabitants remained.

A little more to the southward, at Dor, around Mount Carmel, at Nahalal, Endor, Megiddo, Taanach and Bethshan, all around the plain of Jezreel, the Israelites were unable to exterminate the aborigines.

Again, at the south we find the Philistines in possession of the sea - coast from Joppa southwards. And more inland we have the Gibeonite colony at Gibeon, Kirjath-Jearim and Beeroth; while Gezer, Ajalon, and Jerusalem itself were not by any means Israelite towns.

Lastly, at the extreme south, we find the Amorites inhabiting the mountainous regions to the south and south-west of the Dead Sea.

18. In fact, on carefully examining the map of Palestine, and also the history of the Israelites as given us in the Bible, it is surprising to see what a slight hold they must have had upon the ' Promised Land.'   The sacred writers are most emphatic in pointing out that the Israelites did not drive out the people before them as they had been commanded.

19. Professor Sayce, speaking of Southern Palestine, says: ' It is, therefore, clear that the predominant type of population in that part of Palestine in the time of Rehoboam was still Amorite.   The Jew held possession of Jerusalem and Hebron, and the towns and villages immediately surrounding them; elsewhere he would appear to have formed a subordinate element in the population.'—' Races of the Old Testament,' p. 112.

20. It is highly probable that in many places where for a short time after their invasion the Israelites were predominant, the aboriginal population gradually reasserted themselves, and finally ousted the invaders. Such a state of things is constantly occurring. We see it in Europe and in England ; and the picture presented is a very fascinating one. We see a superior race seizing upon the lands of an inferior one, and for a little time apparently effacing it ; but slowly and surely the con-quered race begins to assert itself, perhaps the longer period during which it has been acclimatized rendering it fitter to survive. And as the members of such a race linger on, so also do their beliefs surviving in folklore superstition and custom, again and again cropping up with marvellous vitality.

21. There is perhaps one respect in which the ethnology of Palestine very nearly resembles that of Great Britain. When the Israelites came into Palestine the Amorites were being driven up into the hill-country bordering on the Dead Sea. It is probable that they had been much more widely spread over the country in former times, but that by degrees other in-vading nations had gradually forced them into the hill-country, though it is not likely that

the Amorites were the aborigines of Palestine.

22. In Great Britain it is supposed that the aborigines were a short, dark, ' Iberian ' race. The next comers were the Goidels, a red-headed people. They appear to have driven the Iberians into the mountains ; but after some time the Brythons, the next comers, appear to have in their turn driven the Goidels into the mountains, where they to some extent amalgamated with the Iberians. There are competent ethnologists who maintain that the Iberian race is gradually reasserting itself both on the Continent and in this country, while Professor Sayce points to the preponderance of ' dark ' whites over ' blonde ' whites in Palestine as a very strong argument against the fair - haired Amorites being the aborigines of that country.

23. The existence of an aboriginal race is noticed in what is supposed to be one of the earliest books of the Bible. The description in the Book of Job shows the aboriginal conquered race to be regarded with that feeling of contempt and dislike with which such races always seem to be regarded.

24. In complaining of his destitute condition, Job says (xxx. 1-9):

' But now they that are younger than I have me in derision,
  Whose fathers I had disdained to set with the dogs of
    my flock.
Yea, the strength of their hands whereto should it profit
    me.
Men in whom vigour is perished.
They are gaunt with want and famine ;
They flee into the wilderness, into the gloom of waste-
    ness and desolation.
They pluck salt wort by the bushes,
And the roots of the broom are their meat.
They are driven forth from the midst of men ;
They cry after them as after a thief.
In the clefts of the valleys must they dwell,
In holes of the earth and of the rocks.
Among the bushes they bray,
Under the nettles they stretch themselves.
They are children of fools, yea, children of men of no
    name.
They are outcasts from the land,
And now I am become their song.'

25. In whatever country, and of whatever people, this is written, the description is remarkable for its well-drawn picture of the inferior race hunted away from the dwellings of their conquerors, hiding in the jungles and secluded valleys, their speech unintelligible, and their presence odious to their masters.

26. May we not, therefore, assume that there were dwelling amongst the Hebrews in Palestine the remains of several nations belonging to different races—for instance, the Hittites, a

Turanian or Mongoloid race; the Amorites, probably a Kelto-Libyan race; and the Edomites and Bedawin, a Semitic race; and perhaps others? Also that these people, being in such proximity to the Hebrews, introduced and perpetuated their customs and superstitions among them; and that it is therefore necessary in discussing the idolatry and superstitions practised among the Hebrews, to seek for their ethnic origin in the various races which formerly possessed Palestine.

CHAPTER II.

THE RELIGION OF THE SOIL.

27. WE very seldom find in the Old Testament a distinctive and detailed account of any heathen ceremony. It is not to be expected that we should do so. To practise divination and witchcraft, and to offer human sacrifices, were all classed together equally as 'abominations,' without any discriminating the shades of guilt incurred by performing such practices. It is therefore only from scattered notices that we must draw our inferences.

28. From such notices we find mention made of the following (amongst other) pagan symbols, customs, and rites:

1. Human sacrifice.
2. A stone pillar or raised stone as an altar.
3. An Ashera or wooden symbol of the god.
4. A graven image.
5. A tree alongside the altar.
6. Eating raw flesh.
7. Immoral practices attending the worship.

8. Women worshipping without men.
9. A sun image.
10. The image of a calf.
11. A high place.
12. Worshipping the sun towards the east.
13. Burning incense to the Queen of Heaven.
14. Pouring out libations to the Queen of Heaven.
15. Making cakes to worship the Queen of Heaven.
16. Saluting or worshipping sun, moon, or stars.
17. Burning incense to Baal.
18. Horses in honour of the sun god.
19. The chariot of the sun.
20. Incense burnt on the housetop.
21. Women weeping for Thammuz towards the north.
22. Passing through the fire.
23. Divination.
24. Witchcraft.
25. Enchantment.

29. We may, however, at once note that the majority of the above items of superstition survive to the present day, in some form or another, in the folklore of Great Britain. If, therefore, they are survivals from early Semitic times, when we meet with them at the period of the Kings, then they must surely be Semitic survivals when we meet with them in Scotland or Devonshire. But if, on the other hand, it can be shown that some of them are found amongst the remnants of the pre-Aryan populations of England and India, then we may fairly assume that these symbols and customs are of pre-Semitic origin in Palestine.

30. If this is so, then we must be prepared to find among the superstitions of Palestine the remains of a pre-Semitic aboriginal cult, a religion of the soil, such as we find traces of in Great Britain and India. But this will not be all. We must also expect to find traces of the Amorites and the Hittites, and latterly the Assyrio-Babylonians. They belonged to distinctive races, and would each have their own superstitions. But ought we to be surprised if the Amorite trace, though distinctive in its features, does not include many items in the foregoing list? I think not. The Amorites were probably not in possession of Palestine for long. They were a warlike intruding race, and when dispossessed of their territory by the next comers, would not probably leave any of their kinsmen behind to perpetuate their superstitions, but would migrate in a body to some other locality, and remain distinct from their adversaries. That the Hittite and Assyrian influence would be largely represented is only to be expected. They were probably the introducers of a highly sensuous worship, and one which was immensely popular, and therefore we must expect their influence to be largely felt.

31. When we examine the list of customs

and rites, etc., bearing the above facts in mind, we may classify it, I think, as follows:

CLASS I.

Relics of pre-Semitic ritual connected with the worship of the reproductive powers of nature.

1. Human sacrifice.
2. Stone pillar or raised stone as altar.
5. Tree alongside altar.
6. Eating raw flesh.
7. Immoral practices attending worship.
8. Women worshipping without men.

CLASS II.

The worship of the heavenly bodies.

9. A sun image.
10. The image of a calf.
11. A high place.
12. Worshipping the sun towards the east.
13. Burning incense to the Queen of Heaven.
14. Pouring out libations to the Queen of Heaven.
15. Making cakes to worship the Queen of Heaven.
16. Saluting or worshipping the sun, moon, or stars.
17. Burning incense to Baal.
18. Horses in honour of the sun-god.
19. The chariot of the sun.
20. Incense burnt on the housetop.
21. Women weeping for Tammuz towards the north.
22. Passing through the fire.

CLASS III.

23. Divination.
24. Witchcraft.
25. Enchantment.

32. It will be noticed that items 3 and 4 are not included in the above classification. As regards No. 3, the Ashera, or wooden symbol of the god, this is probably a development from the stone pillar (No. 2). When the stone pillar, which was originally merely a rude stone, developed into a stone altar, it was felt that something was needed to represent the god. The rough stone would then be supplanted by a stake, perhaps at first rudely carved; in time this would be felt to be unworthy to represent the god, and so eventually would develop into No. 4, the graven image.

33. Let us now proceed to examine Class I. which we have described as 'Relics of pre-Semitic ritual connected with the worship of the reproductive powers of nature.'

Professor Robertson Smith, in his 'Religion of the Semites,' p. 320, gives the following as an instance of the oldest known form of Arabian sacrifice: ' The camel chosen as the victim is bound upon a rude altar of stones piled together, and when the leader of the band has thrice led the worshippers round the altar in a solemn procession accompanied with chants, he inflicts the first wound, while the last words of the hymn are still upon the lips of the congregation, and in all haste drinks of the blood that gushes forth. Forthwith the whole company fall on the victim with their swords, hacking off pieces of the quivering flesh, and devouring them raw with such wild haste that, in the short interval between the rise of the day-star, which marked the hour for the service to begin, and the disappearance of its rays before the rising sun, the entire camel, body and bones, skin, blood and entrails, is wholly devoured.'

34. A few pages further on, Professor Robertson Smith shows that the sacrifice of a camel was merely the substitution of a camel for a human victim, and that in the earliest times a fellow-tribesman was offered, not an animal.

35. I have taken this instance as it deals with several of the items mentioned in our list, namely : 1, human sacrifice ; 2, a stone altar ; 6, eating raw flesh ; 16, special regard for a star. But we will, I think, find that the ceremony in question is not a Semitic one at all, as it tallies almost exactly with non-Aryan festivals in India, and the survivals of such festivals in the folklore of Europe.

36. First let us examine a South Indian village festival, cited in 'Ethnology in Folklore,' p. 22; and as the evidence afforded by this festival is of such importance, I must summarize it at some length :

It is common to Southern India. The goddess is adored in the form of an unshapely stone covered with vermilion. A small altar is erected behind the temple of the goddess to a rural god, Potraj. The pariahs act as priests on this occasion, and the shepherds and low-caste people take part in it as well as the Brahmins, and the non-Aryan low-caste people occupy the foremost places during the festival. The priest is armed with a whip, to which divine honours are paid. The sacred buffalo had always been allowed to roam about the village, but on the second day of the feast it was seized and its head was struck off and placed in front of the shrine, with one foreleg in its mouth. Around were placed cereals, a plough, etc. The carcase was then cut up, and each cultivator buried a piece in his field. The blood and offal, mixed with food, were then put into a basket, with the pieces of a kid which had been hewn in pieces. One of the low-caste men present took the basket on his head and, running off, flung the contents on all sides as an offering to the evil spirits. On the third day those families who had vowed animals brought them to be slaughtered. On the fourth day low-caste people made their offerings. On this day, as also on the previous one, many women walked naked to the temple covered with leaves or boughs, and surrounded by their female friends. On the fifth day, a procession went to the temple. A lamb concealed close by was struck with the whip by the priest, who was then bound with his hands behind his back. He was then led to the lamb, which had been rendered insensible. He seized it with his teeth and ate into its throat. When it was dead, a dishful of the meat was given him, into which he thrust his face. His hands were then untied and he fled. The rest of the party went to the temple, and grain was distributed for sowing. The heads of some of the animals offered were distributed to certain persons, and a scramble took place for the remainder. They were then carried off to be buried in the fields. A procession next took place round the boundaries of the village, the head of the buffalo being carried in the front. Universal license prevailed; the pariahs insulted the Brahmins, the dancing women leaped on their shoulders, and the foulest language was used. At the temple of the goddess of the boundaries, the head of the buffalo was buried, and all dispersed.

37. Let us next look at a description of human sacrifice which was offered until quite

lately amongst the Khonds, another tribe of Southern India.

The first three days were spent in indescribable orgies. The victim has been washed and made to fast. She is then led from door to door, taken into the forest and fastened to a flower-decked pole, thirty or forty feet high, surmounted by a peacock—the emblem of the sun. She (the victim) is crowned with flowers, and the people worship her. At nightfall they rush forward to touch her, and tear her clothes off, each striving to obtain a piece. She is then left all night tied to the pole. Next morning is the great day. With great rejoicings the village turns out to take part in the festival. The priest utters certain invocations, then; seizing a hatchet, he approaches the victim. He loosens her from the stake, stupefies her with opium, then breaks her elbows and knees with the back of the hatchet. There were various modes of slaughter. According to one rite, the victim's head was thrust into a cleft bamboo, which was drawn together by an assistant. The crowd then rushed forward and tore her to pieces with their nails and knives. Each husbandman buries a piece in his garden, or hangs it on a stick over the stream which waters his land. This has to be done at once, for after sundown the flesh loses its efficacy. The head, entrails, and skeleton are burnt, and the ashes scattered to the winds or mixed with the corn for sowing. —'Primitive Folk' (Reclus), chap. vi.

38. We may here note that in Sweden there is a tradition that in the olden time people were accustomed, on the first day of spring, to immolate a living child on a great heap of stones (a cairn), and dance around during the livelong night, to the sound of drums and bassoons.— 'Peasant Life in Sweden' (Lloyd), p. 233.

39. At Khol, near Delhi, we have the survival of some such barbarous ceremony. In the *Mission Field*, April, 1891, there is a description of the worship of a non-Brahmanic cult belonging to the non-Aryan aborigines of the country. The object of worship is a fetish called Bhairou or Bhairoba; it is usually a rough stone smeared with oil. At Bâs Dodâ, three miles from Khol, the stone is set up under a large pipal tree. The foot of the pipal tree has been built round. On the building, a mass of mortar stands with a gash in the front. Over the gash an iron trident protrudes to hold lights which are kindled at special times. This place was once the scene of fearful orgies. 'The fisherman caste of Delhi were formerly wont to bring one of their young unmarried girls on the occasion

of the great *mela,* and marry her to Bhairon.
What this means may be imagined. The poor
girl invariably died within the year.'

40. In Buchanan's ' Journey from Madras,'
reviewed in the *Monthly Review,* 1811, vol. lxv.,
p. 264, we read of the Baydaru that the proper
god of the caste is Trimula Devaru, to whom
a celebrated temple is dedicated. It is an
immense mass of granite on the summit of a
small hill. Under one side of it is a natural
cavity which is painted red and white with
streaks of reddle and lime. In this cavity is
placed a rude stone as the emblem of the god,
and it is attended by a priest, or pujari, of the
caste called Satanana. To this place all the
Baydaru of the neighbourhood once a year
resort. The pujari then dresses some victuals,
and having consecrated them by placing them
before the idol, he divides them among the
people.

41. At this point it is worth while calling
attention to a festival described in the *Monthly
Review,* vol. v., 1791, p. 545, in a review of
Mariti's travels in Cyprus. 'The Nezeires or
Nazarenes are a sect of Christians. Among
the festivals which they observe is one which
they call that of the Womb, on which day they
prostrate themselves before the women and

52496

embrace their knees with an appearance of the deepest veneration. On this and other festivals, when assembled in their place of worship, the windows are shut, the lights extinguished, and the most unbridled licentiousness takes place.'

42. Let us now turn to Livonia. In the *Monthly Review*, vol. xxx., 1799, p. 368, in a review of ' Tooke's View of the Russian Empire,' we read : ' Every year nine days before the feast of St. George, or, as they call him, St. Yurgen, in the night great multitudes of boors of both sexes and of all ages from all the adjacent parts assemble here ' (at an ancient wall near Felmcastle), ' sometimes to the amount of several thousands, kindle a fire within the enclosure of the wall, into which they throw offerings of various kinds, such as yarn, flax, wool, bread, money, etc., at the same time depositing all manner of waxen figures in the little apertures that seem to have served for windows. Round the fire sits a circle of beggars, who have the care of keeping it up, and for their trouble partake of the offerings. Of all the sights in the world this is surely the most ludicrous. All the barren women of the country round dancing stark-naked about these old walls ; others eating and drinking with noisy festivity, many more run-

ning in frisky gambols about the wood and followed by young men playing all sorts of tricks and talking all manner of ribaldry. Hitherto it has not been possible to put down this strange licentious meeting; in the meantime all the circumstances of it seem to show that it is derived from the days of paganism. The offerings, the fire, the dancing, the licentiousness, are manifest proof of it.'

43. Next we have an instance from Western Europe. Near Callac, in Brittany, is situated the village of St. Bulac. On the day of the village festival there is a procession of men and women carrying candles and wearing as few clothes as possible. They afterwards finish up with a dance and a fair. Very close to this village are certain prehistoric stones. There is a superstition that if a barren woman comes at dead of night and rubs her bare bosom against one she will have children.— *English Illustrated Magazine*, 1885-6.

44. We may now examine two English survivals which are very instructive, and are very near akin to some of the very archaic forms of these agricultural festivals which we have been describing.

45. At King's Teignton in Devonshire a lamb is drawn about the parish on Whitsun Monday in a cart covered with garlands of

lilac, laburnum, and other flowers, when persons are requested to give something towards the animal and attendant expenses. On Tuesday it is killed and roasted whole in the middle of the village. The lamb is then sold in slices to the poor at a cheap rate. The origin of the custom is said to be as a sacrifice for water.—' Ethnology in Folklore,' chap. ii.

46. At Holne, near Dartmoor, is a field of about two acres, the property of the parish, and called the Ploy Field. In the centre of this field stands a granite pillar (menhir) six or seven feet high. On May morning, before daybreak, the young men of the village used to assemble there, and then proceed to the moor, where they selected a ram lamb, and after running it down brought it in triumph to the Ploy Field, fastened it to the pillar, cut its throat, and then roasted it whole, skin, wool, etc. At mid-day a struggle took place, at the risk of cut hands, for a slice, it being supposed to confer luck for the ensuing year on the fortunate devourer. As an act of gallantry the young men sometimes fought their way through the crowd to get a slice for the chosen amongst the young women, all of whom, in their best dresses, attended the Ram Feast, as it was called. Dancing, wrestling, and other games, assisted by copious libations

of cider during the afternoon, prolonged the festivity till midnight.—' Ethnology in Folklore,' chap. ii.

47. There is a parallel custom in China. ' On the day that the sun enters the fifteenth degree of Aquarius, which is the commencement of spring, a feast is held in honour of husbandry and celebrated husbandmen; numerous figures in connection with this art are carried in procession, and among them a huge cow of clay, so large that forty men can with difficulty carry it; behind the cow, whose horns are gilt, is a young child with one foot naked and the other covered, representing the genius of labour and diligence. The child strikes the earthen cow without ceasing with a rod, as if to drive her forwards. She is followed by all the husbandmen with musical instruments, and by companies of masquers. At the governor's palace this cow is broken in pieces, and the fragments, with a number of small cows, taken from the larger one, are distributed to the multitude, whilst the governor makes a discourse in praise of husbandry.'— ' Anthropological Studies ' (Buckland), p. 96.

48. In our list of pagan symbols and customs (No. 31) we classified as pre-Semitic ritual connected with the worship of the reproductive powers of nature—

1. Human sacrifice.
2. Stone pillar or raised stone as altar.
5. Tree alongside of altar.
6. Eating raw flesh.
7. Immoral practices attending worship.
8. Women worshipping without men.

49. But we find by the study of the various customs which have been described that there appears to be a prehistoric ritual which includes many of the items alluded to, and also includes others not mentioned in our list. We may therefore by combining some of the items, omitting one, and adding others not found therein, but which appear in more than one of the customs described, arrive at the items of a prehistoric ritual from which these various customs and their folklore survivals seem to have descended.

50. The prehistoric ritual would be as follows :

(*a*) Place of ceremony—a raised stone.
(*b*) Symbol of Deity—a rude stone.
(*c*) Decoration of victim with garlands, etc.
(*d*) Killing of victim by community.
(*e*) Struggle for flesh by members of community.
(*f*) Time of ceremony—before daybreak.
(*g*) Festivities attending cremoney.
(*h*) Sacred power of flesh.
(*i*) Origin of ceremony—to ensure fertility.
(*j*) Ceremonies performed by women in a state of nudity.

When this ritual has been adopted by an intruding race, we may find :

(*k*) Aborigines act as priests.

51. If we tabulate the ceremonies we have been examining, we shall be able to see at a glance how all the festivals compare :

		R. Smith, Arabian Sacrifice ... No. 33	South Indian Festival ... No. 36	Khond Festival ... No. 37	Swedish Tradition ... No. 38	Bhairou Festival ... No. 39	Baydaru Festival ... No. 40	Nazarene Festival ... No. 41	Livonian Festival ... No. 42	Breton Custom ... No. 43	King's Teignton Festival ... No. 45	Holne Festival ... No. 46	Chinese Festival ... No. 47
(a)	Place of ceremony—a stone pillar	x		x	x	x				x	x	x	
(b)	Symbol of Deity—a rude stone...		x			x	x			x			
(c)	Decoration of victim			x							x		x
(d)	Killing by community	x		x	x	o					o	x	x
(e)	Struggle for flesh	x	x	x			o					x	o
(f)	Time—before daybreak...	x			o							x	
(g)	Festivities attending ceremony		x	x	x	x	x	x	x	x	x	x	x
(h)	Sacred power of flesh...		x	x	o							x	o
(i)	Origin—to ensure fertility		x	x	x			x	x	x	x	x	x
(j)	Ceremonies performed by nude women		x					o	x	o			
(k)	Aborigines as priests		x			x			o				

o Only traces remain of this.

52. On looking through this table, we must at once be struck by the recurrence of four of the items, viz., *e, g, h, i,* in the South Indian, the Holne, the Khond, and the Chinese ceremonies; the recurrence of *d, e, f, g, h, i,* in the Holne, the Khond, and Chinese ceremonies; the recurrence of *d, g, h, i,* in the Holne, Khond, Chinese, and the Swedish ceremonies; and the recurrence of *a, d, f, g, h, i,* in both the Holne and the Swedish ceremonies. We also notice that the South Indian and the Holne ceremonies together contain every item except *c,* and out of the nine items have four in common.

53. The examination of the above ceremonies, then, is, I think, quite sufficient to show that the sacrifice, which has been described as the earliest known form of Arabian sacrifice, is not a Semitic form at all, but is merely a form of sacrifice which has once been practised over a very wide area by a prehistoric aboriginal race, and which has left its traces in the folklore and agricultural customs of Western Europe and Southern India, as well as China and Arabia.

54. When, therefore, we read of the 'feasts of blood,' of 'devourers of man's flesh' (Wisd. xii.), of the land being 'polluted with blood' (Ps. cvi.), of pillars which were to be dashed in

pieces, and of serving gods under trees (Deut. xii. and xvi.), and of idolatrous festivities, we may, I think, see in them not survivals of an early form of Semitic religion, but traces of that prehistoric ritual which has lingered on even to our own day in European countries.

55. Before leaving the tabulated statement, however, let us examine thoroughly the Livonian custom, which will, I think, show the close connection which undoubtedly exists between many items in Classes I. and II. in our list of pagan customs, etc., mentioned in the Bible.

56. In the first place, we notice that this ceremony is connected with the feast of St. George. Now, Baring Gould, in his 'Curious Myths of the Middle Ages,' has shown the close connection that exists between that saint and both Tammuz and Osiris. Both these gods are sun-gods. The worship of Tammuz or Adonis was known at Jerusalem in the time of Ezekiel (viii. 14), and, with Adonis, the goddess Astarté was also worshipped as the 'Queen of Heaven.'

57. We must also bear in mind that the festival of Astarte was celebrated in the month corresponding to April, so that the Livonian festival and the Astarte festival were celebrated within a few days of each other. We can

further note that in Jeremiah xliv. 19 the
expression 'make cakes to worship her' (the
Queen of Heaven) is translated in the margin
of the Revised Version, 'make cakes to pourtray
her,' the meaning probably being that sacred
cakes bearing the image of the goddess were
made to be eaten. In Egypt the pig, which
represented Set, the slayer of Osiris, was sacrificed symbolically in his image made of paste.
(*Nineteenth Century*, Sept., 1886, p. 437.) Professor Robertson Smith identifies Adonis himself as the swine-god (p. 392).

58. Without straining the evidence, we may,
I think, in the waxen figures deposited in the
window openings, see the remains of some such
symbolical figures which would be deposited in
the window openings, just as the women who
wept for Tammuz sat at the door of the temple.

59. The above may probably represent the
higher type of sun-worship ; but the dancing of
the naked women, the eating of the cakes, and
the licentiousness are probably traces of the
older sacrificial ritual which we have just been
considering. The circle of beggars who feed
the fire and partake of the offerings are probably
the last survival of the aboriginal priesthood,
who, during the period of a festival, had always
been chosen to officiate by the incoming race.

CHAPTER III.

60. In considering Class II. of our list, the worship of the heavenly bodies, we may first note what Professor Robertson Smith says: 'Among the Semites the worship of sun, moon, and stars does not appear to have had any great vogue in the earliest times. Among the Hebrews there is little trace of it before Assyrian influence became potent, and in Arabia it is by no means so prominent as is sometimes supposed.'—'Religion of Semites,' p. 127.

61. It is well also to bear in mind that the early Assyrian religion was probably derived from the Accadians, who were a people well versed in astronomy; and it is to their influence we may therefore ascribe the prominent place which the worship of the heavenly bodies held in the Assyrian religion.

62. It is, of course, admitted that neither the

Accadians nor the Assyrians were the *originators*
of the tendency to worship the heavenly bodies,
which appears among the Semites. The worship of the sun, moon, and stars is a worship
which probably comes naturally to any uncivilized people, and thus we get sun and moon
myths all the world over. But when we come
to a distinct or elaborate ritual or certain
persistent ritual acts occurring in different areas,
we may then, not unnaturally, look for a
common origin.

63. The Bible evidence quite bears out the
view which is stated above as to the prominence
which Assyrian influence gave to such worship
among the Hebrews. The earliest mention of
the worship of the heavenly bodies in the Bible
is probably Job xxxi. 26, 27, and it is merely an
allusion to the practice. The same may also be
said of the two places where it is mentioned in
Deuteronomy, namely, chaps. iv. 19 and xvii. 3.
But when we examine the allusion in 2 Kings
xvii. 9, 10, 16, 17, we notice a reference to high
places, pillars, Asherim on hills and under
trees, the image of a calf, Baal worship, passing
through the fire, divination, and enchantment.
Now, the pillars and Asherim under trees belong
to what we have termed the religion of the soil.
How is it that they are all mentioned together?

64. That question can be answered, I think, somewhat in this manner. The foreign intruding religion could not afford to ignore the old sanctuaries of the aborigines. At those sacred spots the new rites were celebrated in conjunction with the old, and alongside the Asherim were erected the sun images.

65. This adaptation of the sacred rites to the new religion is by no means confined to Palestine. Most holy wells in our own country, now dedicated to Christian saints, have come down with all their sanctity from pagan times, and many a pagan altar has been reconsecrated for the use of Christians. At the meeting of the Oriental Congress held in 1892, Professor Ramsay read a paper on the ' Persistent Attachment of Religious Veneration to particular localities in Asia Minor,' in which he showed that certain sites which now obtained their sanctity from some Mohammedan saint, had in connection with them a strange and secret ritual, which was clearly older than Mohammedanism and Christianity, and was probably the survival of some ancient pagan cult.

66. But what of the passing through the fire which we find among the Hebrews? It is not part of the ritual we have examined, neither is it Assyrian in its origin. The practice appears

too often in the folklore of Northern Europe
to be of Assyrian origin ; it seems rather to belong to the blond race. Can we not see here
the influence of the Amorites, who probably
entered Palestine from the north-west, and
drove the aborigines into the hills, being themselves subsequently driven there after them ?

67. Professor Sayce has remarked ('Races of the
Old Testament ') that the area in which cromlechs are found corresponds with that occupied by
the ' blond ' race, of which the Amorites formed
part ; and that cromlechs similar to those found
in parts of Britain are also found in those parts
of Palestine occupied by the Amorites. If there
are similar monuments, is it surprising to find
similar customs ?

68. We are told (2 Kings xxi. 6) that Manas-
seh made his son to pass through the fire, and
(verse 11) that he did wickedly above all that
the Amorites did. ' Bodin informs us from
Maimonides that it was customary among the
Amorites to draw their new-born children
through a flame, believing that by this means
they would escape many calamities.'—Burder,
' Oriental Customs,' p. 319.

69. This practice was found both among the
Phœnicians and Carthaginians. Now, it is said
that the Phœnicians probably came from South

Arabia, but it is not probable that they brought the fire sacrifice with them, as it is not common in Arabia.   Is it not likely that the Phœnicians were really a dominant caste who adopted the rites they found practised in the land to which they came, and that the Amorite influence, or the influence of the blond race in Northern Syria, is responsible for the practice of passing children through the fire ?   The same influence would be felt in Carthage.   Cromlechs of the type found in Britain and Palestine are also found in North Africa, and the Kabyles, who are of the blond race, inhabit the site of Carthage.   The Tyrian settlers, therefore, who came to Africa would find there a race to whom the practices they had learnt in Northern Syria would be familiar, and who would therefore cause the invaders to continue them unaltered.

70. In Carthage we find that the sacrifice of children was performed at a great image with a bull's head and human body.   The image was of metal, and made hot by a fire kindled within it, and the children laid in its arms, rolled from them into the fiery lap below.   Rabbi Simeon says, in speaking of the statue of Moloch outside Jerusalem : ' It was a statue with the head of an ox, and the hands stretched out as a man's, who opens his hands to receive something from

another. It was hollow within. . . . The child was placed before the idol, and a fire made under it till it became red-hot. Then the priest took the child, and put him into the glowing hands of Moloch, and, lest the parents should hear his cries, they beat drums to drown the noise' (Burder, 'Oriental Customs,' p. 134). We may also here note that at the spring festival to Astarte, called the 'Brand Feast,' or 'Feast of Torches,' huge trees were burnt with the offerings suspended on them.—' Phœnicia,' p. 116.

71. Now, in the folklore of Northern Europe, we have many instances of passing children through the fire, we have survivals of the image to which the children were sacrificed, and we have remains of the 'Brand Feast' in the Yule log and Maypole.

72. The following extract from the *Gentleman's Magazine* of 1811, will give a very good idea of the survivals to be found of this form of human sacrifice.

' The people of this district (Callander, Perth) have two customs, which are fast wearing out, not only here, but all over the Highlands, and therefore ought to be taken notice of while they remain. Upon the first day of May, which is called Beltan or Beltein Day, all the boys in a township or hamlet meet in the moors. They cut a table in the green sod of a round figure, by casting a trench in the ground, of such circumference as to hold the whole company. They kindle a fire and dress a repast of eggs and milk in the consistency of a custard. They knead a cake of oatmeal, which is toasted at the embers against a stone. After the custard is eaten up, they divide the cake into so many portions, as similar to one another as possible in size and shape, as there are persons in the company. They daub one of these portions over with charcoal till it be perfectly black. He who holds the bonnet is entitled to the last bit. Whoever draws the black bit is the devoted person who is to be sacrificed to Baal, whose favour they mean to implore in rendering the year productive of the sustenance of man and beast. There is little doubt of these inhuman sacrifices having been once offered in this country, as well as in the East, although they now pass from the act of sacrificing, and only compel the devoted person to leap three times through the flames, with which the ceremonies of this festival are closed.'

73. In 'Peasant Life in Sweden' (Lloyd), p. 259, we read: 'St. Hans' Eve (Midsummer Eve) is the most joyous night of the whole year. In parts of the country, more especially

in the provinces of Bohus and Scania, and in districts bordering on Norway, in which country Balder was worshipped, it is celebrated by the frequent discharge of firearms, and also by huge bonfires, formerly called "Balder's Balar," symbols of the obsequies of that god—whose body was consumed on an immense funeral pyre—which are kindled at dusk on hills and eminences, and throw a glare of light over the face of all the surrounding country. It is remarkable that it is still the custom to dance around and jump over and through these fires, reminding one of the ancient feasts of Baal or Moloch, when the worshippers are described as passing through the fire to Moloch.'

74. The following, from the *Gentleman's Magazine* of 1795, refers to the survival in Ireland. 'The chief festival in honour of the sun and fire is upon the 21st of June, when the sun arrives at the summer solstice, or rather begins its retrograde motion. I was so fortunate in the summer of 1782 as to have my curiosity gratified by a sight of this ceremony to a very great extent of country. At the house where I was entertained, it was told me that we should see at midnight the most singular sight in Ireland, which was the lighting of fires in honour of the sun. Accordingly, exactly at

midnight the fires began to appear, and taking the advantage of going up to the leads of the house, which had a widely-extended view, I saw on a radius of thirty miles all around the fires burning on every eminence which the country afforded. I had a further satisfaction in learning from undoubted authority that the people danced round the fires, and at the close went through these fires, and made their sons and daughters, together with their cattle, pass through the fire, and the whole was conducted with religious solemnity.'

75. In *Folklore*, 1891, p. 135, we read: ' The Stromberg, with Druidical remains and traditions, is a noted place for the worship of the sun. Until recently, perhaps at the present day, every midsummer night saw the historic *cérémonie de la roue enflammée* observed on its summit. On St. John's Eve a colossal sheaf was manufactured of straw, contributed from neighbouring farms, and fixed on a big pole as on a pivot, that it might turn round and round. After the sounding of the Angelus some hundreds of men marched up to the mountain-top, carrying lighted torches. No women were allowed to take part. When quite dark the sheaf was set on fire and turned rapidly round, so as to present the appearance of a huge fiery

wheel—symbol of the sun. Similar customs, not unlike the old Celtic Beltan or Belstein, survive likewise in Alsace and the Black Forest.'

76. From India also we get evidence of a fire-festival. Burder, quoting Sonnerat, mentions as an instance of the supersitition of the ancient Indians, 'the grand annual festival holden in honour of Darma Raja, and called the Feast of Fire, in which, as in the ancient rites of Moloch, the devotees walk barefoot over a glowing fire extending forty feet . . . some carrying their children in their arms, and others lances, sabres, and standards.'

77. In the *Mission Field*, April, 1892, the Rev. W. Horsfall, writing from Province Wellesley, in the Malay Peninsula, says: ' But here the Hindus keep a festival which is now forbidden in India. This is the fire-festival. . . . In front of the temple was an immense fire of glowing charcoal about thirty feet in length and ten feet in breadth. A large oblong hole is dug some inches deep, and the fire is made in this. The heat and the fumes of this furnace make it quite unapproachable. . . . The priest, bearing on his head a large goblet, wreathed with flowers and filled with sacred water, steps forward. One almost holds

one's breath with horror to see this man walk through this veritable pool of fire, and immediately followed by the others. . . . At some of these festivals in the provinces I am told that little children are carried through the fire by their deluded fathers.'

78. Here, then, we have in Scotland, Ireland, and Sweden clear traces of sun-worship, accompanied by human sacrifice or passing children through the fire, and in Germany the same ceremonies, but without the passing through the fire. In India also we have among the Hindus—the most organized portion of the population—a similar fire-festival, in which children are carried through the flames.

79. The blond race, which Professor Sayce calls the Kelto-Libyans, have had a home in all these countries. We may, therefore, fairly assume that the superstitious practices referred to, which are found in these countries, belong to the 'blond' race, and that the same practices in Palestine, where this race had settled, were brought there by them.

80. As regards the image of Moloch, Brand, in his 'Popular Antiquities,' says : 'On the subject of giants, it may be curious to add that Dr. Milner, in his " History of Winchester," 1798, speaking of the gigantic statue that

enclosed a number of human victims, among the Gauls, gives us this new intelligence concerning it: "In different places on the opposite side of the Channel, where we are assured that the rites in question prevailed, among the rest at Dunkirk and Douay, it has been an immemorial custom on a certain holiday in the year to build up an immense figure of basket-work and canvas to the height of forty or fifty feet, which, when properly painted and dressed, represented a huge giant, which also contained a number of living men within it, who raised the same and caused it to move from place to place. The popular tradition was that the figure represented a certain pagan giant, who used to devour the inhabitants of these places, until he was killed by the patron saint of the same." Have not we here a plain trace of the horrid sacrifices of Druidism offered up to Saturn or Moloch, and of the beneficial effects of Christianity in destroying the same?'

81. But it is not only in France that we find the giants. Giants form a great feature in the folk pageants of England, and some of the pageants are held on the same day that the Beltan festival is celebrated in Ireland and Germany. 'Plott, in his "History of Oxford-

shire," mentions a custom (yet within memory) at Burford, in that county, of making a dragon yearly and carrying it up and down the town in great jollity on Midsummer Eve, to which, he says, not knowing for what reason, they added a giant.'—Brand, p. 176.

82. ' In King's " Vale Royal of England," we learn that Henry Hardware, Esq., Mayor of Chester in 1599, for his time altered many ancient customs, as the shooting for the sheriff's breakfast, the going of the giants at midsummer, etc., and would not suffer any playes, bear-baits, or bull-bait.'—Brand.

83. ' Puttenham, in his " Arte of English Poesie," speaks of midsummer pageants in London, where to make the people wonder are set forth great and uglie giants marching as if they were alive.'—Brand, p. 177.

84. We see, then, that the ' going of the giants at midsummer ' is an ancient custom in 1599; and when we see an ancient custom repeated in France, Oxfordshire, Chester, and London, we are right in searching far back for its origin. And I venture to think that these midsummer giants can best be accounted for by their being a survival of the idols before which children were sacrificed in the remote past.

85. As regards the Brand Feast which took place at the spring festival among the Phœnicians, we may note that the Beltan festivals are found on both May Day and Midsummer Day, and that on both these days we find that trees or decorated poles have an important place in folklore.

86. In his ' Popish Kingdom ' Googe mentions that on the Feast of St. John the Baptist (June 24) the youths and maidens kindle bonfires and dance, decorated with garlands and herbs, and that they cast them into the fire. Also in the *Gentleman's Magazine*, 1820, it is said that traces of these rites are still found in South Wales. At Llangeneth, in Glamorganshire, at the festival of the patron saint, which falls on June 24, we find that the garlands, the pole, the dances, and the bonfires are still retained.

87. In Acerbi's ' Travels through Sweden,' published at the beginning of this century, attention is called to a custom observed on Midsummer Day, namely, the placing of ' shrubs and flowers at the doors of great houses, as they do in France on the 1st of May.' On that day the king and royal family come to the park, where they take up their abode in tents for the remainder of the month.

A festival is then held by the soldiers, who erect poles in the camp adorned with cypress and various devices.

88. In 'Peasant Life in Sweden,' we read that the great attraction of the evening on Midsummer Day 'is the Maj Stang,' one of which in rural districts is raised at midsummer in nearly every large hamlet. This consists of a straight spruce pine divested of its branches. At times hoops, and at others pieces of wood placed crosswise, are attached to it at intervals; whilst at others it is provided with bows, representing a man with his arms akimbo. From top to bottom not only the Maj Stang itself, but the hoops, bows, etc., are ornamented with leaves, flowers, slips of various cloth, gilt egg-shells, etc., and on the top of it a cock or large vane, or it may be a flag, commonly white or red, on which is inscribed the name of the Apostle John or that of the hamlet and date. Some of these votive pillars, if the expression may be used, are thought to be symbolic of sun-worship, as, for instance, the garlands being made to represent triangles, and wheels with spokes, these forms being known to represent the sun, at least among the Egyptians and Phœnicians. The wheel with rays being still the sign of the sun, and the obelisk, or pointed

pillar, is also supposed to have had the same
signification. The raising of the ' Maj Stang,'
which has been previously decorated by the
maidens of the village, is attended with much
ceremony and by the sound of the violin
or other musical instrument, while guns, or
it may be small cannon, are repeatedly dis-
charged. People from all quarters flock to
the ' Maj Stang,' and after forming a great
ring dance around it. Everyone enters into
the amusement, from the old grandmother to
the child of three years old, the unrestrained
wing of gladness being extended over all. The
dance over, for the time at least, they sit down
to the evening repast; and when this is ended,
they either dance again or amuse themselves
as best they may, it being the custom for everyone on this festive occasion to remain up and
moving during the whole night.

89. In England, when the Yule-tree was
being dragged from the forest to the fire, passers-
by used to lift their hats to it as a token of
respect. In Westmorland, on the Epiphany,
at eight o'clock at night, a procession used to
go through the place, led by a man carrying a
tree, every branch of which ended in a light.
The biggest and strongest available was selected
to carry the tree. He was followed by a band,

and many persons joined the train also carrying trees, smaller, but likewise covered with lights. When all the lights on the big tree were burnt out, it was placed in the middle of the village, the people made a circle round it, and then rushed on the tree and tore it to pieces.—*Newbery House Magazine*, vol. i., p. 646.

90. In India we also find a festival in which a decorated pole plays a part. The ancient festival of Bhavani is annually celebrated by the Gopas and all other Hindoos who keep horned cattle. On this feast they visit gardens, erect a pole in the fields, and adorn it with pendants and garlands.—*Monthly Review*, 1793, p. 546.

91. Let us summarize the evidence so far as we have gone. We find, then, a race which, according to ethnologists, was scattered over a very large area. The home of this race was possibly in Europe, somewhat to the north-east, or perhaps slightly to the north of the Black Sea, and from thence the members of this race migrated as far as India, and the southern and eastern shores of the Mediterranean. In the area occupied by this race we find traces of a fire ritual, where persons were made to pass through the flames. In two of the countries known to have been occupied

by this race, we have detailed accounts of the sacrifice of children before a huge image. In other countries where this race were known to have lived, there are traces of these huge images still surviving. We also find in one of the countries, as part of the same worship, the sacrifice of a decorated tree; and we further find that sacred or decorated trees are found in other parts of the same area, as part of the ritual connected with festivities which are still held on the same day as the decorated tree before mentioned was sacrificed.

92. We may, therefore, I think, conclude that the passing through the fire was a ceremony which originated with this race (viz., the blond race), and that where this practice appears among the Canaanites and Hebrews, who occupied Palestine subsequently to the 'blond race,' and when members of that race were still surviving in the land, it was derived from that race or that portion of them known as the Amorites, and was not a practice originally in vogue among the Semitic race to which the Hebrews and Canaanites belonged.

93. When, however, we proceed to further consider the other items which we have classified under Class II., it will not be sufficient merely to eliminate the item passing

through the fire (22), which we have classed as
of Amorite origin, and designate all the other
items as Assyrian. It is quite possible that
horses in honour of the sun-god (18), may also
be Amorite. The horse was sacred to Odin,
and at Rhodes we read of horses cast into the
sea in honour of the sun-god. Rhodes was
occupied by the Dorian Greeks as well as the
Phœnicians, so that the 'blond race' might be
responsible for the sacredness ascribed to the
horse, both among the Scandinavians and
Rhodians.

94. There are, however, some other items
which are not necessarily Assyrian, for instance
the high place (11). This may be, as suggested
in the 'Religion of the Semites,' but the necessary
accompaniment of the transition from blood
sacrifice to fire sacrifice. Then we have the
image of a calf (10). This may be a survival
from early Semitic worship, or possibly from the
pre-Semitic inhabitants especially, as Professor
Robertson Smith says 'the origin of the sacred
regard paid to the cow must be sought in the
primitive nomadic life of the Indo-European
race' ('Religion of the Semites,' p. 280). If this is
so (and several other facts mentioned in the
same work point very strongly to the like conclusion), we may see in the ox-headed image of

Moloch another link to connect the Carthaginian sacrifice with the Amorites.

95. But we must here estimate, if possible, the effect of the amalgamation of the religion of the soil, which would be celebrated at the sacred sites, with the Assyrian worship of the heavenly bodies. To do this, let us picture to ourselves one of these ancient sacred sites. A rude stone smeared with blood, and alongside it a tree, are at first the only visible symbols. Then, it may be, fire sacrifice is introduced. The stone is used for the altar of burnt offering, and alongside of it an Ashera (a wooden pillar) is erected, to be smeared or painted in place of the stone. Then foreign influence comes to be felt, and the burnt offerings are more numerous. The old altar is found inconvenient, and a ' high place ' is built. A king or queen—like Jezebel —introduces the new (Assyrian) religion on a large scale. The Ashera is carved to represent the god (the Baal); in time the image of a calf is substituted. The priests of the Baal increase, a ritual is introduced, and a sun image. Turning towards the east, they worship the sun, they burn incense before the image of the god, they pour out libations to the ' Queen of Heaven,' they burn incense to her, and make sacrificial cakes in her honour. Very shortly

this worship is introduced into the cities, incense is offered to the heavenly bodies from the house-tops, and their worship is even introduced into the temple at Jerusalem. The women weep for Tammuz at the north gate of the temple, and men worship towards the east with their backs to the temple, while at the gates can be seen the horses and chariot of the sun, which, as the symbols of an older religion, and one un-fashionable with the priestly caste, had not yet been taken within the more sacred enclosure.

96. We shall thus be able to classify chrono-logically the items in Class II. as follows:

22. Passing through the fire.
18. The horses of the sun.
19. The chariot of the sun.
11. The high place.
10. The image of a calf.
17. Burning incense to Baal.
16. Saluting or worshipping sun, moon, or stars.
9. The sun image.
12. Worshipping the sun towards the east.
14. Pouring out libations to the Queen of Heaven.
13. Burning incense to the Queen of Heaven.
15. Making cakes to worship her.
20. Burning incense on house-tops.
21. Women weeping for Tammuz.

97. This classification, however, does not profess to be the chronological order in which these customs and symbols originated, but

only the order in which they may have reached Palestine.

98. We may, therefore, in concluding this chapter on the worship of the heavenly bodies, briefly sum up the conclusions arrived at :

(*a*) The worship of the sun, moon, and stars was not common among the early Semites, though it may have been prac-tised to some slight extent among them.

(*b*) There is no trace of it among the Hebrews until they were brought into contact with the nations of Palestine.

(*c*) The first form of such worship amongst the Hebrews was derived from Amorite sources.

(*d*) The later developments of such worship were the result of Assyrian influence.

CHAPTER IV.

DIVINATION, WITCHCRAFT, AND ENCHANTMENT.

99. In the Book of Deuteronomy we read, 'When thou art come into the land which the Lord thy God giveth thee, thou shalt not learn to do after the abominations of these nations. There shall not be found with thee anyone that maketh his son or his daughter to pass through the fire, or that useth divination, one that practiseth augury or an enchanter, or a sorcerer, or a charmer, or a consulter with a familiar spirit, or a wizard, or a necromancer' (Deut. xviii. 9-11).

100. It is, then, very clearly stated that the practice of divination, enchantment, and sorcery was known to the former pagan inhabitants of Palestine. But in the verses we have just quoted we find classed together both the causing children to pass through the fire and also the practice of divination and enchantment. It does not, however, follow that any nation

which practised one of these customs would practise them all; certainly not to any great extent.

101. For instance, we have classed the passing children through the fire as an Amorite custom ; it does not therefore follow that that nation was skilled in enchantment. It is much more likely that the Hittite influence was responsible for the enchantments, sorcery, and magical formulæ in use in Palestine. The Hittites were a 'Turanian' race, and probably akin to the Accadians, who were much given to magic, and many years before the Israelites had come out of Egypt, or even gone there, the Hittites had been a power in Palestine and Syria.

102. As the Hittites had been in Palestine, we must expect to find traces of their influence, and I think we may rightly ascribe to their influence the practice of magic and enchantment. Students of religion class Shamanism— or the idea that the whole universe swarms with malevolent beings, who must be propitiated by the repetition of magical formulæ and the aid of the enchanter—as the distinctive feature of the Turanian race.

103. But if we proceed to examine some of the instances given us in the Bible of divination

and witchcraft, we may be able to trace in them the influence of the various races among which they may have originated, or, at any rate, by whom they were introduced amongst the Hebrews.

104. We will first take Joseph's cup. 'Is not this it in which my lord drinketh and whereby he indeed divineth ?' said Joseph's servant to the eleven brethren, when he discovered the cup in Benjamin's sack.   It is not, however, at all likely that Joseph brought this superstition from his father's home.

105. Burder on this subject says: 'Julius Serenus tells us that the method of divining by the cup among the Abyssinians, Chaldees, and Egyptians was to fill it first with water, then to throw into it their plates of gold and silver, together with some precious stones, whereon were engraved certain characters, and after that the persons who came to consult the oracle used certain forms of incantation, and so, calling upon the devil, received their answers several ways ; sometimes by articulate sounds, sometimes by the characters, which were in the cup, rising upon the surface of the water, and by this arrangement forming the answer, and many times by the visible appearing of the persons themselves about whom the oracle was

consulted. Cornelius Agrippa tells us likewise that the manner of some was to pour melted wax into the cup, wherein was water, which wax would range itself into order, and so form answers according to the questions proposed.'

106. As a more modern instance of the use of the cup, we read : ' When Norden was at Derri in the farthest part of Egypt, in a very dangerous situation, from which he and his company endeavoured to extricate themselves by exerting great spirit, a spiteful and powerful Arab, in a threatening way, told one of their people, whom they had sent to him, that he knew what sort of people they were, that he had consulted his cup, and found by it that they were those of whom one of their prophets had said, that Franks would come in disguise and, passing everywhere, examine the state of the country, and afterwards bring over a great number of other Franks, conquer the country, and exterminate all.'

107. The divination of Joseph by means of the cup is not, however, I think, an instance of Hebrew superstition. The superstition of the divining cup appears in ancient Eastern traditions, and the custom was probably not an Egyptian one. If we remember that, according to some Egyptologists, Joseph's sojourn in

Egypt was during the time of the Hyksos kings, and that these kings came from Northern Syria, and also that the statues of these kings prove them to have been of a Turanian Hittite, almost Chinese, type, we can quite understand that they would have brought with them to Egypt a good deal of Accadian superstition and magic, including the divining cup.

108. Another instance of divination given us in the Bible is divination by arrows. It is mentioned in Ezek. xxi. 21: 'For the king of Babylon stood by the parting of the ways, at the head of the two ways, to use divination, he shook the arrows to and fro, he consulted the teraphim, he looked in the liver.' Jerome on this passage says : ' The manner of divining by arrows was thus: They wrote on several arrows the names of the cities they intended to make war against, and then, putting them promiscuously all together into a quiver, they caused them to be drawn out in the manner of lots, and that city whose name was on the arrow first drawn out was the first proceeded against.' —Burder, ' Oriental Customs.'

109. In Sale's Koran, Preliminary Discourse, he says : 'The arrows used by them for this purpose were like those with which they cast lots, being without heads or feathers, and were

kept in the temple of some idol, in whose presence they were consulted. Seven such arrows were kept in the temple of Mecca; but generally in divination they made use of three only, on one of which was written, " My Lord hath commanded me," on another, " My Lord hath forbidden me," and the third was blank. If the first was drawn they looked on it as an approbation of the enterprise in question; if the second they made a contrary conclusion; but if the third happened to be drawn they mixed them and drew over again till a decisive answer was given by one of the others.'

110. Herodotus says (iv. 67): 'Soothsayers among the Scythians are numerous, who divine, by the help of a number of willow rods, in the following manner: When they have brought with them large bundles of twigs, they lay them on the ground and untie them; and having placed each rod apart, they utter their predictions; and whilst they are pronouncing them they gather up the rods again and put them together again one by one. This is their national mode of divination.'

111. In ' Anthropological Studies,' Buckland, p. 151, we read: ' It is at all events matter of history that arrows marked with certain signs **were** used in divination among the Scythians,

Chaldæans, Arabs; and Tacitus says among the Germans also.' And on p. 157: 'That a very intimate connection subsisted between the arts of divination by rods or arrows, the casting of lots, and the primitive alphabets, cannot, I think, be doubted. It is a significant fact that just in those regions of Asia where arrows were principally used in divination, there we find the cuneiform or arrow-headed characters in use. It would, moreover, appear that both divination and the primitive alphabets originated with that very early semi-civilized race, which seems to have spread over the whole world prior to the rise of the Aryan supremacy, a race generally, although perhaps not very correctly, denominated Turanian, and which has certainly left traces in the language, religion, and customs of almost all nations quite alien to Aryan culture.' . . . 'Maurice, in his "History of Hindustan," says Naga, in its primary sense, signifies *diviner*. The pre-Aryan population of India and the Scythians, pre-eminently diviners, doubtless belonged to this race, as did also the Etruscans, according to Canon Isaac Taylor, and they likewise were noted as soothsayers and diviners. Lenormant traces an underlying Turanian population in Chaldæa, Persia, and among the Eskimo.'

112. I have dwelt somewhat fully upon this custom, as it might be said that the prophet Ezekiel was merely ascribing to the King of Babylon a practice which was common among the Hebrews. But after examining the evidence it must, I think, be admitted that the practice of divination by arrows was not an instance of Hebrew superstition. The evidence all seems to point to a Chaldæan or Turanian origin for the custom, and as we have no evidence that it was practised among the Hebrews before the Captivity, we may trace its origin to their contact with the Babylonians.

113. The next instance of divination is mentioned in Hosea iv. 12, ‘ My people ask counsel at their stock, and their staff declareth unto them.’ Robertson Smith says, ‘ Religion of the Semites,’ p. 179 : ‘ But in Hosea iv. 12 the “ stock ” of which the prophet's contemporaries sought counsel can hardly be anything else than the Ashera. . . . As the next clause says, “ and their rod declareth unto them,” it is commonly supposed that rhabdomancy is alluded to, *i.e.*, the use of divining rods. And no doubt the divining rod, in which a spirit or life is supposed to reside so that it moves and gives indications apart from the will of the man who holds it, is a superstition cognate to the belief in sacred

trees ; but when " their rod " occurs in paral-
lelism with " their stock," or tree, it lies nearer
to cite Philo Byblius, who speaks of rods and
pillars consecrated by the Phœnicians and
worshipped by annual feasts.   On this view
the rod is only a smaller Ashera.   Drusius,
therefore, seems to hit the mark in comparing
Festus's note on *delubrum,* where the Romans
are said to have worshipped pilled rods as
gods. . . . Was the omen derived from the
rod flourishing or withering ?   We have such
an omen in Aaron's rod, and Adonis rods set
as slips to grow or wither seem to be referred
to in Isa. xvii. 10.'

114. If in this passage in Hosea rhabdomancy is referred to, I think it is highly im-
probable that it originated among the Hebrews.
This form of superstition is known in Scythia,
Assyria, Palestine, Greece, Etruria, and Rome,
and according to Lenormant it is extremely
developed among the Finns.   We may therefore, I think, class it as a superstition kindred
to divination by arrows, already described, and
one which was of Turanian origin, and introduced into Palestine by the Assyrians, or
perhaps the Hittites.   If, however, the rod is
only a smaller Ashera, it is quite possible that
it may be of Amorite origin.   Chapter x. in

Buckland's 'Anthropological Studies' deals somewhat fully with the subject of divination by rod and arrow, and on page 149 we read : 'In almost all civilized lands we have legends of trees to which miraculous virtues are ascribed. The oaks of Dodona and of the Druids, the ash of Scandinavia, America, and Britain, are examples of this.' If, therefore, the Ashera was made of the wood of a sacred tree, the superstition might very possibly be Amorite, as the 'blond race' are known to have such trees, rods made from which were supposed to be endued with mysterious properties.

115. There is very slight mention of enchanters and enchantments in the Old Testament. We read first of Pharaoh's magicians. But as we are more particularly examining Hebrew superstition we need not dwell on Egyptian magic.

116. The next mention of enchantment is the case of Balaam. The King of Moab finding that he was unable to prevail against the Israelites, sent for Balaam. This Balaam 'the diviner,' as he is elsewhere called, came from Mesopotamia, perhaps Chaldæa. The inhabitants of the Euphrates valley were at this time, and until long afterwards, renowned for their skill in magic and enchantment, and

it was probably for this reason, though also possibly because he was supposed to be acquainted with the 'manner' of Israel's God, that Balaam was sent for.

117. Balaam probably used some Accadian enchantment. After the seven altars had been built and the seven bullocks and seven rams offered thereon, it seems that the diviner went to 'seek for enchantment.' This no doubt meant that he went to the top of the hill to mutter his formulæ or seek for an augury from something he might see. At any rate, it is very certain that it was not a Hebrew ceremony. The Moabites were probably Semites, and when their gods had failed and other means of defence were exhausted, they fell back on the enchantments of this foreign diviner for their protection.

118. The only mention of enchantment among the Hebrews is (2 Chron. xxxiii. 6) where Manasses is said to have used enchantment and witchcraft; but as this verse gives a very general description of Manasses' superstitions, the remarks made in § 101 apply to his case.

119. When we come to consider the witchcraft of the Bible, we find various commands forbidding the practice, but only one specific

mention of a particular witch, namely the one at Endor.

120. In Exodus xxii. 18 we find the commandment that no witch was to be permitted to live. The reason appears to be because witchcraft, or the use of magical rites, was practically a renunciation of the Deity. Professor Robertson Smith shows that in a well-regulated state the person who availed himself of unauthorized worship and rites was looked upon as striving to get some advantage for himself in which his fellow tribesmen could not share, and in doing so he had to pass by the God of his people and have dealings with some strange god. And if we adopt this view we can quite see that the witch or person who had dealings with some other power was practically a denier of the God of Israel, and by the Mosaic code was worthy of death.

121. In considering the case of the witch of Endor, let us again refer to Mr. Gomme's ' Ethnology in Folklore.' We find in chap. iii. set out at length the evidence to show that witchcraft is caused by the presence of an aboriginal or uncivilized race alongside of a superior and intruding race.

122. Now it is at least remarkable that the town where this witch resided is one where

the former inhabitants were not expelled. It is therefore just in this neighbourhood where, according to the modern evidence, we would look for the presence of persons reputed to practise witchcraft. If she belonged to one of these former races the superstitious Hebrews would look upon her with a certain amount of reverence, and Saul, feeling that he had angered the God of his own people, would inquire of this woman, whom he would look upon as the representative of other gods who might be disposed to help him in his desperate straits.

123. The case of Saul and the witch has been repeated again and again amongst imperfectly civilized peoples dwelling amongst people of another religion. When their own deities do not answer, or the appointed channels of access to such deities appear to be failing, then they betake themselves to the wizard, the magician, the conjurer, or the priesthood of another race, the magician and wizard being the folklore representatives of such priesthood. Lane, in his 'Modern Egyptians,' draws a very accurate picture of such a state of affairs. He says : 'It is a very remarkable trait in the characters of the people of Egypt and other countries of the East that Muslims, Christians, and Jews adopt each

other's superstitions, while they abhor the more rational doctrines of each other's faiths. In sickness the Muslim sometimes employs Christian and Jewish priests to pray for him ; the Christians and Jews in the same predicament often call in Muslim saints for the like purpose. Many Christians are in the frequent habit of visiting certain Muslim saints here, kissing their hands, begging their prayers, counsel, or prophecies, and giving them money and other presents.'

124. May we not, then, without straining the evidence, ascribe the witchcraft mentioned in the Old Testament to the influence of the former inhabitants of the land, many of whom were left among the Hebrews, and whom the ignorant among the Hebrews would regard with a superstitious fear, as being in league with the gods of the land? The same kind of influence is exercised by alien races now; why should not it be exercised then ?

125. If we, then, sum up the conclusions stated in the former pages we find that the various practices and superstitions were derived as follows :

(*a*) The divining cup ; found in Egypt. Brought there by the Hyksos, who were a Turanian race.

(*b*) Divination by arrows; found in Babylon and also

among the pre-Aryan peoples of Europe and India.
Probably a Turanian superstition.

(*c*) Divination by rods, or rhabdomancy ; found in
Palestine. Probably brought there by the Hittites,
as it is known among the pre-Aryan races of Europe
and India. It is probably also a Turanian superstition.

(*d*) Divination by the ' Stock,' or small Ashera ; found in
Palestine. Brought there by the Amorites. A
superstition of the blond race.

(*e*) Magical formulæ ; found in Mesopotamia. Probably
Accadian or Chaldean in origin.

(*f*) Witchcraft ; found in Palestine. Caused by the
mythic influence of the former inhabitants, viz., the
Hittites, Amorites, Canaanites, etc.

CHAPTER V.

CONCLUSION.

126. THE bearing of the foregoing evidence upon the study of the Old Testament appears to be that we must be prepared to lay far more stress upon the influence exercised upon the Israelites by those members of the aboriginal races which remained amongst them, and also upon the survivals from those races which we find amongst the Israelites.

127. When they first came into Palestine, and partially drove out the former inhabitants, we must not suppose that this horde of strangers who had shown such a desire to practise the idolatrous customs of those nations with which they had come in contact in the wilderness, would immediately settle down in a strange land where many of the former pagan inhabitants still remained without adopting some of their customs.

128. It is very probable that a great many of

the Israelites, when first occupying Palestine, felt very much as the Samaritans did at a later period, when they were brought into a strange land.   Man, when in a not very highly civilized state, has a tendency to endue everything about him with life.   Each mountain, each valley, each river, has its guardian spirit, and the less a man knows about any object, the more potent is the influence he ascribes to it.   An Israelite who had not a firm trust in Jehovah would be tempted to think that in the new land upon which he had entered there were gods to be propitiated.   And like the Samaritans before referred to, they would seek for some of the former occupiers to act as priests, and teach him the ' manner ' of the ' God of the land.'

129. An   Israelite, while   a   member of   a victorious   army,   having   the   support   of   his comrades, and being led by a well-tried leader who had an unbounded faith in the power and goodness of Jehovah, would be a very different being to the man who, with a few other villagers, had been allotted a few fields in an out-of-the-way village, surrounded, it may be, with thickly-wooded mountains, in whose recesses dwelt some fierce tribesmen, who had been dis-possessed of their inheritance by the intruding Israelites.   Surrounded on all sides by unknown

dangers, the faith of a timid man would be sorely tried, and before long he would very likely be tempted to come to terms with his enemies natural and supernatural. And who would be more likely to know the best way to propitiate the invisible powers than the members of the outcast race who knew their haunts, their 'manner,' and the ritual acts necessary to render them a valid worship?

130. If this is admitted—and we must remember that the evidence of an outcast race elevated to the priesthood is not confined to Palestine, very strong evidence being found in Britain and India—we can quite understand how the customs and superstitions of the former race were introduced among the incoming one. To account for the presence of idolatry and heathen customs among the Hebrews, we need not, therefore, formulate theories of their origin, which are contrary to the traditions which that race have carefully preserved from the very earliest times, and theories which will not square with all the facts.

131. The evidence of folklore cannot be neglected in considering the Old Testament narratives. A purely literary criticism must have its uses, but if the conclusions arrived at by such a criticism are contradicted by the

evidence of ethnology and folklore they should be received with caution.

132. It is often said that as religious instincts are conservative, therefore all heathen customs discovered among any people are survivals of a former religious condition of such race. Such a theory seems plausible, but it is contradicted by facts. Nations borrow religious customs more easily than develop them; and when we meet with a race (like the Hebrews) which has been brought into contact with other races, and which has lived side by side with them for generations, we must not be surprised if this race has borrowed and assimilated the ritual and religious customs of its neighbours. The surprise would be if it had not.

133. Let us, then, in conclusion briefly sum up :

(*a*) There is evidence to show that an aboriginal race can hand down their religious customs and superstitions to an incoming race. The former inhabitants of Palestine appear to have handed down such customs and superstitions to the Hebrews.

(*b*) Among the customs so handed down appears a prehistoric ritual connected with the worship of the reproductive powers of nature. Traces of such ritual are found over a large area and show signs of being of great antiquity.

(*c*) There are also customs which may be traced to the Amorites, as survivals of such customs are found in countries which have been occupied by races kindred to the Amorites. Assyrian influence is also clearly seen during some portion of the history of the Israelites.

(*d*) The superstitions, practices, divination, and enchantment can be traced back to the influence of particular races, while the belief in witchcraft is to be ascribed to the presence of the various conquered races.

(*e*) The religion of the Hebrews was one of great morality, and when the nation fell into idolatry they were acting contrary to the principles of their religion, and were adopting the lower religious standard of the former inhabitants of the land, members of such former races surviving amongst them and perpetuating the lower standards of religion.

INDEX

THE END.